# NEPALESE VEGE
# AND HEALTH FOOD RECIPES

## by
## Angela Dietrich

**NEPALESE VEGETARIAN AND HEALTH FOOD RECIPES**
Angela Dietrich

*Published by:*
PILGRIMS BOOK HOUSE (Kathmandu)

PILGRIMS BOOK HOUSE
*(Distributors in India)*
B 27/98 A-8, Nawabganj Road
Durga Kund, Varanasi-221010, India
Tel: 91-542-2314060, 2312456
E-mail: pilgrims@satyam.net.in
Website: www.pilgrimsbooks.com

PILGRIMS BOOK HOUSE (New Delhi)
9 Netaji Subash Marg, 2nd Floor
Near Neeru Hotel,
Daryaganj,
New Delhi 110002
Tel: 91-11-23285081
E-mail: pilgrim@del2.vsnl.net.in

*Distributed in Nepal by:*
PILGRIMS BOOK HOUSE
P O Box 3872, Thamel,
Kathmandu, Nepal
Tel: 977-1-424942
Fax: 977-1-424943
E-mail: pilgrims@wlink.com.np

First Edition 1997
Copyright © 1997
All Rights Reserved

*Typesetting, Layout & Bookcover by* Sherap Sherpa
*Black & White illustrations by*
Baburaja Dyola, Bara Arts, Lagankhel, Lalitpur

ISBN: 81-7303-061-8

*Printed in India*

Jyapuni, Newar farming woman, peeling potatoes for a *bhoj*,
a Newari feast

Food preparation for a *bhoj*

Onions, maize an garlic cloves drying in the sun

Village damsels pounding beaten rice or *Chura*

Drying rice grain and red chillies on the village square in Bungamati

Serving guests at a *bhoj*

Main dishes served at a *bhoj*

Modern Nepalese kitchen

Old fashioned Newari kitchen in Bungamati

Drying maize and garlic cloves on an old Newari house

Puja vessels (sukunda, kalas, aunti, etc.)

## INTRODUCTION

This modest collection of dishes emerged out of a five-year period spent in Nepal. As an anthropologist, I was naturally intrigued by the culinary aspects of people's ethnic identities and so these dishes are intended to reflect Nepal's ethnic and caste mosaic, ranging from the northern Tibeto-Mongolian through to the more indianised, southern Terai region. Having lived mostly in the Kathmandu Valley, the cuisine of the Valley's original inhabitants, the Newars, is, naturally, predominant. There is, not surprisingly, a greater number of dishes gleaned from their unique cuisine, blending northern and southern influences, with a strong ceremonial, tantric flavour. Being a vegetarian who occasionally eats fish, and in addition, conscious of the necessity of maintaining a healthy diet, has caused me to be especially selective when it came to the choice of recipes. To my delight, though, I discovered that the Newars, in common with many other Nepalis, are also keen on maintaining the kind of diet in which health is not sacrificed to taste. Nevertheless, I took the liberty to introduce certain modifications, for example, in that I tended to go easy on the spices and oil.

I myself have contributed two recipes to this cookbook: one is what I hope is an improved version of the Nepalese national dish, *dal-bhat*, and my own idea of what can be tastefully done with left over *khicheri*, under Nepali inspiration. *Khicheri*, as I soon discovered living in Nepal, is a necessary food for a stomach easily upset by semi-tropical conditions. In putting together the Newari recipes, I would like to acknowledge the help of a few talented friends, one of them, Ama Shrestha, a lecturer in Home Economics, who was also knowledgable about the religious and social background of certain dishes. My second contributor was Amita Shakya, a very skillful handicraft artisan and excellent cook, whose recipes I often had an opportunity to sample since I was living in her father's house in Patan.

The Newars have a very complex science of nutrition and food categorisation which is regretably, beyond the scope of this slim volume to dwell upon. Suffice it to say that they have developed an elaborate food culture not only suited to the palate, but also based largely upon Ayurvedic concepts of healthy ingredients, combinations of certain foods with select spices, suited to specific seasons and individual constitutions. These concepts were, as Ama indicated when she gave me her recipe for millet cake, originally propagated and articulated through the medium of ritual. With growing modernisation, however, this culture appears to be fast diminishing, without something correspondingly sophisticated and nourishing to replace it with. Thus the increasing incidence, for example, of the famous Newari wedding feast or *bhoj*, relying entirely upon Indian food, even sans the spices, to make this insipid alternative to traditional Newari cuisine, ostensibly more `palatable' for the westernised guests.

Fortunately, however, there are still people who wish to preserve and cultivate their own heritage, culinary and otherwise, to make compilations like the present one possible. Thanks to them I am sure the recipes in this book will provide people unfamiliar with this culinary tradition with new inspiration for what could well be a refreshingly different approach to food preparation and enjoyment.

The book is divided into three sections, appetisers, main courses and desserts. Since Nepalese generally lack the strictures which many other South Asians who are debarred, mostly for religious reasons from consuming alcohol, are subject to, it is perhaps not surprising that appetisers and snacks are often consumed with country-made liquor. The strong variety is called *rakshi* in Nepali and *ayla* in Newari, and is served, on ceremonial occasions, in beautiful metal decanters. The less potent drink, *chang*, is a home-brewed variety of beer, though it also resembles the new wine produced in Germany, for instance, since it has the same milky colour and consistency, and a similar sweet-sour taste. Both drinks are most commonly made of rice, but can also be produced from millet - especially in the cold season, when people residing in the higher altitudes of Nepal, drink *tomba* out of bamboo containers and straws, made by pouring hot water on fermented, roasted millet. Maize, in its stead, is occasionally utilised for brewing either *chang* or *rakshi* in the villages, in case there is a surplus of this important staple food item.

Most meals, in Nepal, are consumed mainly within the parameters of the immediate family, especially if they involve the serving of white, boiled rice, though if more relatives and friends are included, this is likely to be substituted by *chura* - dry, flat, beaten rice. Though not considered as ritually `pure' as boiled rice, *chura* nevertheless enjoys a strong ritual significance as an essential ingredient on ceremonial occasions. For example, the Newari *bhoj* at which *chura* is served on leaf plates, normally accompanies important ritual events like marriage, birth and death, though there are many others in between. For Newars, more often than not, any occasion is good enough to celebrate and the best way to do it is to cook and serve a huge feast, feeding as many people as their pockets will allow. Besides gaining merit in a religious sense through feeding others, this is the most important way a Newar knows to be sociable and cultivate contacts which may be significant in more ways than one.

The snacks section, reflective of the sociability of the culture from which it originates, possibly exhibits the greatest variety. Newars in particular, can boast of having an elaborate and ceremonial snacks culinary culture. The Newar appetiser par excellence is called *samay baji*, considered a tantric sacramental food. Normally consumed at the end of a ritual, it is a kind of appetiser, or, if substantial enough, it can even be a substitute for a full feast. *Samay* is the same as the Sanskrit word *samaya*, meaning a vow or sacrament and *baji* refers to beaten rice or *chura*. Besides the mandatory *chura*, this snack is normally composed of roasted buffalo meat (in the case of non-vegetarians), black soya beans and black-eyed beans, raw ginger slices, a green vegetable and is sprinkled with puffed rice. However, depending upon the family's preferences, it can also include *woa*, the famous dal pancake, some sauteed potatoes, a hard boiled, spiced duck or chicken egg, dried fish and some sweets, to be washed down with the obligatory small clay container of *ayla*. The basic ingredients are supposed to represent the set of six flavours which are considered, in Newari tantric philosophy, essential at a religious feast or *bhojana*: spicy, astringent, sour, bitter, salty and sweet.

The dishes comprising the section on main courses have been chosen for their representative nature, hailing as they do from various districts of Nepal. Since the country is amongst the poorest nations in the world, it may come as no surprise that the variety is somewhat restricted. However, what is lacking in scope is made up for in wholesomeness, since Nepal also boasts of having some of the hardiest and strongest people on earth, particularly the porters carrying loads sometimes exceeding their own weight. What makes the latter so strong is crucially their diet, as they subsist mainly on finger millet and, in the higher regions, barley, and maize in the lowlands. The majority of Nepalese, though, subsist on the ubiquitous *dal-bhat*, though many visitors may find this combination of steamed rice, a thin dal soup and one or more curries, rather dull with time. This impression is compounded by the fact that the Nepalese people normally have their *dal-bhat* twice a day, once in the morning and again in the evening. It is said that, lacking at least one repast at which *dal-bhat* is served, they feel they have not actually eaten, even if they have had a full meal of something else. Newars, for example, often greet each other in the morning with the question, "have you taken rice yet?"

The dishes featured here have mostly been slightly modified to conform to health food principles calling for a reduction of oil, brown, instead of white, polished rice, less chilli and other spices, and vegetables that have not been overcooked or oversalted, as is often the case in this part of the world. Though the original vegetables are being presented here, similar alternatives, more readily available in the west, have been suggested whenever feasible. However, since the world is rapidly shrinking, many, even very exotic vegetables are increasingly becoming available in most metropolises globally, so it may be worth hunting them out in a delicatessen or large supermarket, which stock foods for a more discerning palate.

The last section, that of sweets, is the shortest, reflective of the generally low priority accorded desserts in Nepalese society. Though formerly, the Newars in particular produced elaborate sweets like *lakhamari* included in this collection, mostly in ceremonial contexts, nowadays, ready-made sweets are sadly replacing them. In general, sweet dishes are, more often than not, served as snacks or even as a breakfast food, rather than to round off a meal. Sweets, in general, are particularly served to honoured guests like a new son-in-law his wife's natal family wishes to pamper so that he will treat essential component of certain ritual food items. In any event, an Indian influence is perhaps more predominant here. However, characteristically, most Indian sweets tend to be too sugary for the non-Indian, so the dishes included in this section have been specifically chosen due to their relatively low sugar content, with the exception of a few obligatory sweets like the proverbial Nepalese *jirhi*. In any event, the white sugar called for in the majority of these recipes can be successfully substituted either by *shakar*, brown, unrefined cane sugar found in certain specialty shops in the old part of Kathmandu or Patan, or by honey, also a healthier alternative to white sugar. In fact, in compiling this cookbook, I have sought to avoid, as much as possible, all `five poisons' from the health point of view, which include white sugar, bleached, white flour, white, polished rice, margarine or vegetable ghee and to a lesser degree, white table salt.

The alternative to white salt in Nepal is *kalo noon*, black or red mineral salt, purchased in rock form and ground to a fine powder to be used in place of ordinary salt. Though called black, once ground, it is in fact, pink in colour, having a characteristic aroma of its own which some people find enhances the flavour of the food, though others not accustomed to it, may find it odd or even unpleasant. Not surprisingly, though, since it is a mineral, it is said to have medicinal properties and is in fact, an important component of Ayurveda. Lacking somewhat in iodine, however, it should perhaps be occasionally substituted with ordinary, iodized table salt, rather than used exclusively. *Kalo noon* is especially advisable for those suffering from high blood pressure or heart disease, who must reduce their salt intake.

On this note, I hope you will enjoy cooking and sampling the recipies included in this modest collection. Perhaps you will also notice the incredible versatility of certain staple food items you may have considered rather mundane, like dal. This mandatory accompaniment to rice in Nepal undergoes phenomenal transformations when it is used to produce savoury doughnuts or pancakes, as a filling for certain vegetables, to make dried koftas called *mashaura* or even as an essential ingredient in sweet dishes. Thus, the book can justifiably advertise itself as both a vegetarian (with the exception of a few fish dishes) *and* health foods cookbook, perhaps unique amongst the available compilations in English language.

Unless indicated otherwise, all dishes are for a minimum of six people.

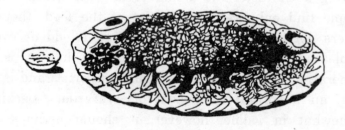

*SAMAY BAJI*

# LIST OF RECIPES

1

## III. SWEET DISHES

SEL ROTI ON CHATTAMARI, LAKHAMARI

## YAMARI
### Sesame Rice Cones

Eight cups of rice flour
Half cup of brown sugar, *shakar* or honey
One cup of brown sesame seeds

*Yamari* was introduced into Nepal by King Anshuvarma during the Lichhavi era. It is usually prepared once a year on the full moon day in November. This day is called *Yamari Punhi*. It is also prepared for children's six-yearly birthday anniversaries (at age six, twelve, etc.). On this occasion, relatives, especially married daughters and sisters, are invited and serve *yamari* as a side dish in a feast or *bhoj*. Children are garlanded, with the number of *yamari* mirroring their ages.

1 Prepare the dough in advance by mixing one and an half cups of boiling water with the rice flour and kneading it, once it has cooled down, for at least ten minutes. Cover with a kitchen towel.
2 Roast dry sesame seeds for five minutes and mix with the brown sugar. Add half a cup of water and simmer for 20 minutes. While cooking, stir frequently until the mass gets sticky. Remove from the stove and let cool for 10 minutes.
3 Mould the dough into rounds, the size of large marbles. Roll out thinly into an elongated, conical shape, joining the edges to form a cone, as depicted on the picture.

4 Fill each cone with a spoonful of the sesame mixture and seal the top with a rice paste.

5 Steam either in a momo-steamer or in an ordinary vegetable steamer for 15 to 20 minutes on medium heat. They can be eaten either warm or cold.

Fillings can be varied: for example, a steamed moong cake can be used, either savoury without any sugar, or sweet. Another filling is *kuwa*, similar to cottage cheese, made by boiling one liter milk until thick and adding one tablespoon of ghee or butter and half a cup of sugar. When cool, the mixture can be used to fill the *yamari* and steamed in the same way.

*YAMARI*

## CHATTAMARI
### Rice Flour Pancakes

Three cups of rice flour or three cups of rice, soaked overnight and pureed in a blender
Split black gram (dal), soaked overnight, skinned and pureed
One cup of cooking oil
Salt to taste

*For filling:*

One small head of cabbage
Three medium-sized onions
Three large-sized potatoes
One teaspoon parsley or coriander, finely chopped
One teaspoon ginger paste
Two tablespoons garlic paste
Turmeric, chilli powder, salt, pepper - one teaspoon each, or to taste

1 Take the soaked dal and remove most of the skins by rubbing together.
2 Mix with the rice flour or rice paste, blend with two to three cups of water to make a batter, which should be slightly thinner than an ordinary pancake batter.
3 Pre-heat a skillet and pour in approximately one teaspoon of oil. Mustard oil imparts a flavour of its own, suitable for savoury pancakes. Soya, peanut or corn oil may be substituted for mustard oil, if you so desire.

4 Make one at a time, using about third of a cup of batter for each thin pancake, which should be about the size of a saucer.

5 After pouring on the batter, cover for about four minutes until fairly firm. Do not turn.

*Chattamari can be either savoury, using the filling below, for a substantial snack or full meal, or served sweet, with butter and either honey or maple syrup and are then suitable as a breakfast food.*

### FILLING:

1 Finely chop potatoes, cabbage and onions and fry together in one tablespoon preheated oil.

2 When half cooked, add spices, and continue sauteeing.

3 At last, add the parsley or coriander and mix, continuing to fry for two to three minutes.

4 Place one tablespoon of the mixture in the centre of each *chattamari* and cook on low heat for five minutes, either open-faced or closed, covered.

*Newars relish this dish with a soya and peanut sauce featured on the following page.*

SOYABEAN PLANT

# SOYABEAN AND PEANUT SAUCE

Half a cup each of dried soyabeans, peanuts, cooking oil, lemon juice and water
One teaspoon parsley or coriander
One teaspoon each of garlic and ginger paste, green or powdered chilli (optional)
Salt and pepper to taste

1 Roast soyabeans and peanuts in a heavy iron skillet over low heat.
2 Blend all above ingredients, with the exception of the lemon juice and fresh parsley or coriander, which should have been finely chopped.
3 Once blended to a fine sauce, add lemon juice and parsley and
stir until well mixed.

*Serve as a condiment with chattamari or as a dip for pakora, tempura or raw vegetables.*

## SEL ROTI
### Rice Flour Doughnuts

*Sel Roti* is a very traditional kind of snack, doubling as a popular breakfast food, which one finds in small tea stalls all over the country. Though it may, at first glance, seem easy to prepare, it may require several attempts to make an adequate version of this typical doughnut. Its circumference is thinner than that of an ordinary doughnut and the fact that it is made out of rice, rather than wheat flour, accounts for its being more filling and substantial than its lighter counterpart.

If eaten as an afternoon snack, *sel* can be served together with *alu-ko-achar* listed further on in this cookbook.

*Sel* is prepared on certain ceremonial occasions in Nepal, notably on Bhai Tika at the end of Tihar, the day on which brothers are being honoured by their sisters by applying a `tika', a red mark made of rice and vermillon, to their foreheads. Tihar falls in late October or early November, just after the celebration of Dasain, which are the major Nepalese Hindu festivals. Dasain commemorates the mother goddesses' victory over the demons represented by the gentle-looking buffalo, which, together with other animals is sacrificed in this festival. During Tihar, a number of animals are worshipped on different days - the crow, dog, cow and ox - by garlanding them and giving them `tika', finally culminating in Bhai Tika.

The ingredients and method of preparation are as follows:

Five cups rice flour
Seven cups water
Three cups sugar
Four cups cooking oil or (non-vegetable) ghee
Half a cup ghee or melted butter

1 Mix the rice flour and half a cup of ghee or melted butter in a bowl and stir for about 15 minutes. Add the water and sugar, and stir well, until it is a smooth mixture, about the same texture as *chattamari*.
2 Put a deep pan, karahi or wok on the stove and heat the ghee or oil. Test it to see if it is hot enough by putting a small amount of the batter in. If it sizzles, it is ready for making *sel*.
3 Take a small amount of batter and fill a pastry maker, with a hole at one end the size of a dime, through which the batter can flow.
4 Release the batter into the oil slowly, making a circle with the circumference of a demitasse saucer. In the event that it is not fully joined or uneven, not to worry. No *sel* is ever a perfect circle.
5 Turn over when nicely browned or reddish in colour, frying on both sides, a process which takes about six minutes in total.
6 Allow the *sel* to drain on paper towels before serving when they are still warm. Cold *sel* should be reheated beforehand since the oil may have developed a rancid taste.

# WOA
## Dal Pancakes

Half a kilogram of split moong or black gram (dal)
One cup of mustard oil
Half a teaspoon of the following spices to taste:
Salt, pepper, garlic and ginger paste, cumin powder or seeds
One bunch of fresh coriander or parsley
For fillings: eggs or keema (minced and spiced goat, lamb, buffalo or beef)

1 Clean and soak dal overnight or for five to six hours.
2 Drain away the water and, in the case of black dal, separate and discard the skins.
3 Grind the dal on a grinding stone for better taste, or liquidize (though not completely) in a blender for more convenience.
4 Mix with the spices and salt and form small or larger pancakes, depending upon the filling or your own taste. Be sure the dal mixture is firm enough to press into pancakes and if not, add some brown, whole-meal flour.
5 Fry on both sides in enough hot oil to surround them.
6 If you are adding fillings, make a slight indentation on one side which has not been fully cooked, add the filling and pour some oil over it. In case you are adding a raw egg, break the egg over a pancake large enough to accomodate it and try not to break the yolk.
7 Turn over when browned and fry until well done. Since you are using raw dal, it is necessary for the *woa* to be well cooked before consuming.

*Woa* is a traditional Newari dish dating back centuries, which is enjoyed on ceremonial occasions or can be served together with drinks before a meal or as a substantial snack between meals. Some people prefer one kind of dal over the other. It is true that the moong is slightly easier to digest than the black gram which, for its part, is the more nourishing kind of dal of the two. It may be important to note that, although for Newars, the preferred oil is mustard, it is quite strong in taste and rather heavy, and therefore you may prefer to substitute a different kind of oil instead.

BHAI TIKA

# FANCY VEGETABLE CUTLETS

Four medium-sized potatoes
One onion and a carrot
One cup finely chopped string beans
One cup finely chopped cauliflower
Two eggs
Half cup bread crumbs
Half cup whole wheat flour
One bunch fresh parsley or coriander
Two green chillies (optional)
One tablespoon ginger-garlic paste
Cooking oil
Turmeric powder, salt and pepper to taste

1 Put potatoes on to boil in their jackets.
2 Finely chop the other vegetables. Sautee the onion, adding the ginger-garlic paste when nicely browned.
3 Add the other vegetables and sautee with the spices until half cooked. Lastly, add the chopped coriander and remove from heat.
4 Drain off the water from the potatoes, peel and mash. Sprinkle the flour on the mashed potatoes, adding a pinch of salt, and blend well.
5 Divide into small balls and flatten each one, putting a bit of the vegetable mixture into the centre. Shape into cutlets, dip in the beaten eggs and roll in bread crumbs.
6 Fry cutlets until golden brown on both sides. Serve hot or cold with tomato sauce or any other sauce of your choice. Soya and peanut sauce is also suitable as a condiment for this dish.

# FISH CHOPS

Any kind of firm-fleshed fish
Two large potatoes
Two medium-sized onions
One egg
One half cup bread crumbs
One tablespoon ginger and garlic paste
Salt, chilly pepper (optional), garam masala, according to taste
One bunch of fresh coriander or parsley
Oil for frying

It can be noted that these chops are a variation on the above, with the addition of fish to replace most of the vegetables. Thus, the method of preparation is quite similar to that of vegetable cutlets.

1 Boil the potatoes in their jackets.
2 Cut up the fish and sautee in a tablespoon of oil or ghee with a bit of salt. When done, remove bones and mash the fish.
3 Grind the onions together with the ginger and garlic. Fry and add the ground spices.
4 Add the fish and stirring well, allow to cool slightly.
5 Mash the potatoes and form into chops. Fill some fish mixture into the centre of each one, dip into the beaten eggs and roll in the bread crumbs.
6 Fry in very hot oil or ghee until nicely browned and serve with a sauce of your choice.

# PINEAPPLE KOFTAS

One medium-sized pineapple
One large onion
Half a cup each of green chillies (optional) and sesame seeds
One large potato
Half a teaspoon salt and red chilli powder (optional)
Two cups of oil

*This is a more exotic variation on the cutlet theme, which derives from Nepal's southern districts. However, since pineapple is being cultivated now more extensively in Nepal, this dish is becoming better known and is eminently suitable as a cocktail snack or as part of a `high tea'.*

1 Chop up the fresh pineapple finely (tinned pineapple is normally too sweet and soggy) and mix in salt.
2 Cook in a sauce pan, having added a bit of water, until done.
3 Cut up and boil potato, either in its jacket or peeled.
4 Mince chillies and mix with mashed potato, sesame, pineapple and spices. Knead well and form into small koftas.
5 Heat oil in a skillet and fry the koftas in the deep oil to cover for about 15 minutes. They can be served either hot or cold, with or without a sauce. Chutney would also be suitable for the koftas, especially as a complement to the pineapple used in this dish.

# BARAH
## Black Gram Doughnuts

Half a kilogram of black gram (dal)
Two medium-sized onions
One bunch of fresh coriander or parsley
One inch piece of grated ginger
One bulb of garlic or suited to taste
A pinch of salt and hing (optional)
One teaspoon cumin powder
Mustard oil or any other kind of cooking oil

*Barah* is a Newari doughnut, which, unlike *sel*, is savoury and not sweet. Though rather tricky to prepare, it is however, well worth the effort, as the result can only be described as nothing short of sublime. Although the ingredients are similar to *woa*, the taste and consistency is entirely different, being lighter and finer. Enjoy as a snack or an appetiser with or without drinks.

1 Soak the dal overnight and then, having separated most of the skins, wash well and drain.
2 Grind either on a grinding stone or liquidize in a blender.
3 Add spices and mix in grated onion, garlic and ginger paste. For an improved flavour, leave it covered for an hour or so to allow the spices to sink in properly.
4 Shape into smallish doughnuts and deep-fry in very hot oil for approximately 10 minutes or until reddish-brown in colour. Again, since the dal is raw it is necessary to fry on both sides.

# HAGO MOONG
## Moong Dal Cake

Half a kilogram of split moong gram (dal)
Two eggs
One cup of any kind of hard cheese like yak or cheddar
Five to six cloves of garlic
One inch piece of grated ginger
One teaspoon of cumin
Salt to taste

This is yet another Newari snack which is particularly healthy and suitable for convalescents when served with warm milk. Unlike the others, this dish is steamed and not fried. Although it appears very simple and rather dry, once you have acquired a taste for it, you will undoubtedly appreciate it as a quick `pick me up' snack.

1 Soak the dal overnight and grind it using the methods indicated for the other dal snack recipes.
2 Grate the cheese and finely grate the ginger and garlic to a paste.
3 Add all other ingredients and mix well.
4 Break the eggs into a bowl, beat and blend into moong mixture.
5 Place this fairly thick mass into a steamer - even a rice-cooker can be employed - and steam for about 20 minutes.
*Hago moong* can be eaten piping hot or cold, with or without a sauce, and is even suitable as a breakfast food, especially since it is nourishing and ungreasy at the same time.

# CAULIFLOWER ACHAR

One large or two small cauliflowers
Five potatoes
Two cups of peas
One green pepper
Half cup brown sesame seeds
One pinch of turmeric
Salt to taste
One cup mustard oil
One teaspoon garam masala

This achar is normally kept in a sealed container for several days and is served in small amounts as a kind of condiment to a curry or eaten with chapatis.

1 Cut up the cauliflower and potatoes into small pieces and parboil.
2 Mix in the peas and finely chopped green pepper, and parboil.
3 Grind the sesame seeds and mix in salt, turmeric and garam masala.
4 Add to vegetable mixture, together with the oil, and mix well.

# KWATI
## 12-Bean Soup

*Kwati* could be considered the most `typical' of all Newar dishes, though most Nepalese cook and relish it, too. Particularly Newars regard *Kwati* as a holy dish and it is offered to gods and goddesses, rendering it particularly suitable for festival occasions. It is also a rich source of protein and thought to possess curative properties. On the festival of Janai Purnima, *Kwati* is prepared in the belief that it will cure people's stomach ailments, which are particularly critical at the end of August, when this festival occurs, due to the monsoon season. *Kwati* is considered good for convalescents and is especially warming on a cold winter's day. The soup is commonly prepared out of pre-soaked beans which can either be sprouted beforehand, left unsprouted, or, more rarely, from a mixture of bean flours. In Newari language, `kwa' means hot and `ti' means liquid and a large variety of beans, traditionally 12, but more often than not, less than that, are employed in its preparation.

Half kilogram of beans: an equal combination of available beans, including moong and other kinds of lentils or dals (Bengal gram, house gram, black gram and red gram); dry peas, red kidney beans, white kidney beans, cow peas, black, brown and white soyabeans.
2 large onions
Half a bulb garlic (depending on one's taste)
One-inch piece of grated ginger
Half a cup of soya, or any other oil of your choice
One tablespoon ghee (optional)

Salt to taste
One teaspoon turmeric
One tablespoon cumin seeds
Chilli powder or fresh chillies to taste

First, decide upon which kind of *kwati* you wish to prepare, either the ground, sprouted or unsprouted variety. In case of the former, all the dried beans must be pulverised, which will produce a consume-type of soup. If you decide on one of the others, the beans will need to be soaked overnight, if not longer. In case you decide to make the sprouted variety, which is actually the healthiest of the three, allow the soaked beans to germinate in a nearly air-tight container, the top of which has been perforated with a few small holes. It will take another 16 to 24 hours to sprout.

1  Drain soaked beans.
2  Heat oil in large saucepan or pressure cooker to smoking stage.
3  Fry chillies (optional) and finely diced onions.
4  Add garlic and ginger paste, then the beans with the turmeric and salt. Fry for 10 minutes, stirring often.
5  Finally, pour in about one liter boiling water and cover, simmering or pressure cooking, until beans are done.
6  Heat ghee in frying pan and add cumin seeds, frying them until they pop, and pour into *kwati*, boiling briefly before serving.
*Kwati* can either be served as a side dish or appetizer, or as part of a full meal, together with brown rice or brown bread and a salad.

# PUMPKIN SOUP

A quarter ripe pumpkin (enough pulp to fill about four cups)
Half a cup of butter or ghee
Four cloves of garlic
One cup milk or cream, depending upon taste (optional)
Half a cup of red dal (optional)
Two chicken or vegetable soup cubes
Salt and pepper to taste
One bunch fresh coriander or parsley

1 Boil the red dal in double the amount of water until it is ready, about 15-20 minutes (optional).
2 Roughly grate the pumpkin pulp, but do not discard the liquid.
3 Melt butter or ghee in a deep saucepan, add garlic and finally, the grated pumpkin.
4 Pour in enough water just to cover (or the dal plus a bit more water) and add the soup cubes, together with the salt and pepper.
5 Simmer gently until done (about 15 minutes), adding the milk or cream last, if a richer soup is desired.
6 Add the finely chopped coriander or parsley at the very end.  In the case of parsley, it may be advisable to simmer an extra five minutes, but if you are using coriander, no more cooking is necessary.

The soup may be served with bread and a salad, if so desired, or as a first course.

# FANDO
## Corn Soup

*Fando* is popular in all parts of the country and is considered a rustic delicacy. Corn is though also used to make pop-corn, dried corn kernels are popped in a clay container, normally heated by a wood fire or coals. Alternatively, corn ears are put directly on live coals for a charcoal-broiled flavour, and eaten as a snack, with chilli powder and salt.

Three cups fresh corn kernels
Two chicken or vegetable soup cubes (optional)
Half a teaspoon each of ground ginger, garlic, cumin powder, turmeric and cumin seeds
One teaspoon salt
One teaspoon butter or ghee

1 Husk and separate the kernels from about five ears of fresh corn.
2 Grind coasely and mix with two cups of water.
3 Pour through a muslin cloth or through a fine strainer, if you would like to elimate the roughage from the corn, in case you are using the ordinary, as opposed to the tender corn variety.
4 Mix with six cups of water in a deep saucepan, add spices and soup cubes, if a stronger flavour is desired.
5 Stir and cover, simmering for 10 minutes.
6 Just prior to serving, pop cumin seeds in the ghee which has been heated in a frying pan, and pour into the soup.

## DAL BHAT TARKARI
Rice with Dal and Vegetables

No Nepalese cookbook can be complete without the most important dish of Nepal, commonly known as `dal-bhat', which is a complete and substantial meal in itself. It can be infinitely varied, ranging from a very basic dish of white rice, dal and one side vegetable, to a more elaborate version which can include one or more meat and vegetables dishes, *achar*, plus an additional bean dish and sweet or plain yoghurt, to round it off. However, in the Kathmandu Valley at any rate, generally one green vegetable must accompany *dal-bhat*, in case it is in season, besides a vegetable curry, often made with *alu*. Potatoes, it should be noted, are not considered a staple food similarly to rice or pasta, but are eaten as a side dish in Nepal. At least once or twice a week, *dal-bhat* may also include a meat curry, consisting of chicken, goat or buffalo meat, or a fish curry, an example of which is included in this cook book.

The *dal-bhat* featured here is my own modified version, since it calls for brown, rather than white rice and the vegetables are less spicy than many Nepalese would prefer them to be. Brown rice, it must be noted, is more nourishing than white *chamal* (Nepali for uncooked rice, whereas *bhat* refers to cooked rice), and therefore, most people find they only need to eat half the amount of brown than they do of white rice. A friend once described the Nepalese penchant for consuming `mountains of rice', which definitely referred to the white variety. Brown rice, though sparingly available in Kathmandu, is not very wide-spread in Nepal as a whole, though I have encountered a similar kind of rice which villagers described as red', while trekking. My own version of *dal-bhat*, in any event, calls for two vegetables, one green and one vegetable curry, including potatoes mixed with a seasonal *tarkari*. Ordinarily, to complement the obligatory green vegetable, the ones used in the curry should not be of the leafy variety, but could be any other kind like aubergine, squash or courgette, for instance.

Two cups of brown rice
One cup of dal (any kind)
Half a cup of oil
One kilogram of seasonal vegetables which can include fresh soyabeans, potatoes, onions, spinach or *rayo* (mustard greens), tomatoes and spring onions
Seasoning and spices: garlic and ginger (one teaspoon each), green or dry chillies, cumin seeds, garam masala, mustard, fenugreek and/or mustard seeds, fresh coriander/parsley
Salt and pepper to taste

1 Wash rice and bring to boil in double the amount of water, plus one teaspoon salt.
2 Turn down to lowest heat when boiling, stirring once, and cover tightly. Brown rice takes normally 40 to 45 minutes to be ready.
3 Wash the dal and cook in double the amount of water, either using a pressure cooker or a saucepan. When done, add one chopped, fried onion, salt and some spices,

chopped tomatoes and fresh coriander and simmer
another five minutes.

4 Prepare the green vegetables by washing and chopping
them up.

5 Simmer in half a cup of water or sautee in one
tablespoon of oil, covering and allowing to cook gently in
their own juice.

6 Add salt and pepper at the end. Spices are not
necessary, but may be added if preferred.

7 Prepare the *tarkari*. First, wash and cut up potatoes
and vegetables, including onions or spring onions.

8 Fry onion until golden brown and add seed spices
(cumin, fenugreek, mustard). Now add chopped potatoes,
vegetables and tomatoes and fry together with other
spices (garlic-ginger paste, powder spices and salt).

9 Add enough water to make a gravy, as it will be eaten
together with the rice.

Nepalese serve each dish in its own container or in a
partitioned metal tray, with the expectation that the
guest will require second helpings of each item. For an
authentic `dal-bhat experience', use your hands instead
of a spoon or fork, by pouring the dal on to the rice,
making it sticky and easier to scoop up.

# MASHAURA CURRY
*Karkalo*-Black Dal Kofta Curry

*Mashaura* is a very different Nepali dish, a kind of dried kofta used as a base for curry or mixed vegetables. It is full of protein and minerals, making it an especially valuable addition to a vegetarian diet. Black gram itself is replete with protein and the vegetable, colocasia, which grows prolifically in the wild all over the Nepalese lowlands, is loaded with minerals and vitamins.

## *Mashaura Koftas*

One kilogram black gram
Two kilograms of *karkalo* (colocasia, a green leaf vegetable)
One teaspoon salt
One teaspoon cooking oil (mustard, soya or any other)
Half a cup of whole meal or rice flour (optional)

1 Soak black gram overnight or for several hours and wash to remove as many of the skins as possible.
2 Blend to a smooth paste, together with the oil and salt.
3 Prepare the vegetable, which is a dark-green, large leaf, by chopping it very finely.
4 Mix with the dal paste to make the koftas, by gradually adding the oil and salt to the vegetable-dal mixture. In case it does not stick properly, sprinkle on some of the flour while mixing.
5 Form into ping-pong sized balls and allow to dry in the sun for two or three days.
6 Store in an air-tight container for future use.

*Mashaura Curry*

Two cups of *mashaura*
Two to three medium-sized potatoes, cut into fours
One cup chopped tomatoes
Two tablespoons mustard oil
One teaspoon ginger-garlic paste
One pinch each of turmeric, black pepper, asafoetida, fenugreek powder
Two teaspoons of cumin
One half cup finely chopped parsley or coriander

1 Pre-soak *mashaura* for 10 to 15 minutes and drain, when ready.
2 Heat oil in a deep saucepan, a karahi or wok.
3 Add dry spices and potatoes and saute over medium heat.
4 Add one cup of water and simmer until done.
5 Now add the tomatoes and ginger-garlic paste.
6 Fry the *mashaura* separately until reddish-brown, remove from heat, and add to potato curry.
7 Simmer gently until the *mashaura* are soft.
8 Sprinkle with the coriander and cover pan briefly, before serving with rice or *dal bhat*.

# KHICHERI
## Dal - Rice Dish

*Khicheri* is particularly useful to know about, especially for people with indigestion, delicate stomachs or dysentry. Hence the usage of moong dal, deemed particularly suitable for coping with these kinds of complaints, along with white, in place of brown rice. However, even if your stomach is of the cast-iron variety, this dish can come in handy as a quick alternative to *dal-bhat*, to be served with raita, for example. It can also be `dolled up' by adding sliced onions mixed with popped cumin seeds, fried in ghee, for improved flavour.

One and a half cups of any kind of white rice
One and a half cups of split moong dal
One teaspoon salt
Two chicken or vegetable soup cubes (optional)
One onion, finely sliced (optional)
One teaspoon cumin seeds (optional)
One tablespoon pure ghee (optional)

1 Clean and wash rice thoroughly.
2 Clean and wash dal and put on to boil in three cups of water.
3 Allow to cook for five minutes before adding the rice, as it will only take 20 minutes for the rice to steam.
4 For a more liquidly, savoury *khicheri*, add the soup cubes and use an additional cup of water.
5 Fry sliced onions, if you wish to add them, together with the cumin seeds in ghee or oil and arrange on top when the dish is ready.

# KHICHERI CROQUETTES

This recipe originated out of a desire for utilizing left-over *khicheri*, in a tasty, constructive manner. *Khicheri* croquettes can be served with a yoghurt-mint, tahini or tomato sauce, and make an excellent main course which combines vegetables with dal and rice.

Three cups of left-over *khicheri*
One cup of corn or chickpea flour (*besan*)
One egg
Half a cup of bread crumbs
One bunch of spring onions
One bunch of coriander or parsley
One bunch of spinach or any seasonal leafy green vegetable
A pinch each of cumin powder, chilli powder, garam masala, pepper
Salt to taste
Half a cup of cooking oil

1 Mix cold *khicheri* with the beaten egg.
2 Add flour gradually to produce a firm mixture.
3 Fold in spring onion, coriander and spinach, which have all been finely chopped, being careful to have squeezed out any excess water.
4 Mix in spices at the end and form into croquettes, about the size of koftas, and roll in bread crumbs.
5 Place croquettes gently into hot oil and turn after five minutes of frying over medium heat.
6 Take out after a further five minutes and drain on kitchen towels.

# PANEER PILAU

Two cups of white rice
Two blocks of paneer (six by six inches)
One half cup ghee
Two medium-sized carrots
A hand full each of raisins, dried dates, almonds (slivers or coarsely chopped), cashew nuts (coarsely chopped), to taste
A quarter cup of fresh peas
Salt and pepper to taste

1 Wash and soak the rice in water for one hour.
2 Cut the carrots into small cubes or match stick sized pieces and simmer in half a cup of water together with the peas for five minutes.
3 Chop up the dried fruit and nuts and fry, either in half the ghee or in a mixture of butter and oil. Keep aside.
4 Heat the rest of the ghee and quick fry the paneer, which has similarly been cut into small cubes, adding the carrots and peas at the end.
5 Add salt and pepper (optional) and mix nicely before adding to the drained rice.
6 Place rice mixture in a saucepan with four cups of water.
7 Bring to boil, adding salt, and simmer gently for about 20 minutes until done.

This festive dish is specially good when consumed with a mushroom curry and tomato *achar*.

# TOMATO ACHAR

Two pounds or one kilogram of tomatoes (preferably juicy, cooking tomatoes, as opposed to the drier, salad tomatoes)
One half cup of fresh (or frozen) peas
One medium-sized green pepper
One green chilli (optional)
Two dried red chillies
One half cup fresh parsley or coriander
One medium-sized onion
One medium-sized bulb of garlic
One tablespoon ground or grated ginger
One half cup cooking oil
Two teaspoons salt
Two teaspoons garam masala
Two bay leaves or *tej pat*

1 Dice or chop up all the fresh ingredients.
2 Put a deep skillet, karahi or a wok on the fire and pour in the oil.
3 When hot, fry the dried chillies until they are black and remove and add the *tej pat*.
4 Fry diced onion briefly, add ginger and garlic cloves which have been sliced in half.
5 Finally, add rest of the spices and fry on low heat, together with the vegetables, for five minutes.
6 Next, simmer for a further five minutes with half a cup of water added, until the tomatoes are nicely mixed with the other vegetables.
7 Serve as a condiment either hot or cold.

Other ingredients may be added to this basic pickle, like raw or only parboiled vegetables (aubergines, carrots, mushrooms), or even hard-boiled eggs cut in half, fish like sprats or prawns, to make it into a curry. Since it advertises itself as an achar', it can be kept in a sealed container for some time before serving.

# PANCHA KWA
## Five-Ingredient Stew

The name `Pancha Kwa' means `dish of five ingredients' in Newari, and is popular amongst all Nepalese people. It is perhaps the most celebrated of Newari food items, besides *Kwati*, and has come to comprise what is considered a salient characteristic of Newari cuisine: the combination of potatoes with fermented bamboo shoots. The delicate flavour of the bamboo shoots (especially if they are still young and tender) which in Nepal are purchased in flat, small pieces, having been sliced off a large bamboo shoot stalk, complements and offsets the potatoes and beans. The dish also has a ritual significance, and comprises a combination of at least some of the five most important kinds of tastes as noted in the case of *samay baji*.

Five large potatoes
Two large onions
One cup pre-soaked black-eyed beans
One cup sliced bamboo shoots
Half a cup of dried, black mushrooms (*shitake* or any other fungus-type of mushroom)
Half a cup of dried white raddish (optional)
One green chilli
One tablespoon of mustard oil
Salt to taste
Pinch of pepper and turmeric
One teaspoon of cumin seeds
Two to three *tej pat*

1 Bring beans which have been pre-soaked at least 4 to 6 hours or over-night, to boil, and while simmering, prepare other ingredients.

2 Slice onion and fry briefly in half the oil, with the *tej pat.*

3 Add spices and potatoes, which have been chopped into cubes.

4 Drain beans when ready (should take 10 minutes in a pressure cooker or half an hour otherwise).

5 Mix the pre-soaked raddish in case you are using it and the pre-soaked mushrooms with the potatoes and combine with the beans in five cups of water.

6 Wash and drain bamboo shoots and fry briefly in the rest of the oil before adding to the stew.

7 Simmer on low heat until ready, about 10 minutes.

*Pancha Kwa* can be served with brown or white rice, as part of *dal-bhat*, or, as the Newars are fond of doing, as a main component of a feast or *bhoj*, with beaten rice (*chura*). Of particular importance for vegetarians is the fact that it contains many essential proteins, minerals and vitamins, rendering it a veritable meal in itself.

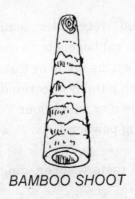

BAMBOO SHOOT

# MOMOS
## Stuffed Dumplings

Perhaps the most popular dish in Nepal besides *dal bhat,* *momos* are very versatile and can be eaten in a soup like its sister, the wanton, steamed or fried, with or without sauces.  They are presumably of Tibetan origin, but as they resemble wantons, could also be of Chinese derivation.  Although the preparation seems arduous, rest assured that the end product will be well worth the effort.  Brown, whole-meal flour can be used in place of white, bleached flour, for a healthier alternative.  Though normally filled with a minced meat and spice mixture, this vegetarian alternative is gaining in popularity. Almost any vegetable is suitable, ranging from mixed, as in this recipe, to plain mashed potatoes, to which grated cheese has been added.  They can also be filled with *kuwa,* for a sweet version, and served with the savoury kind of *momo,* to comprise a full meal.  It is fun to prepare *momos* in a group and invite guests, who are served this delicacy piping hot in batches, as soon as they are taken out of the *momo*-maker, with several tiers.

Mixed, finely diced vegetables (cauliflower, spinach, carrots, mushrooms, cabbage, etc., a quarter cup each)
One large bunch of spring onion or three onions, diced.
Two bunches of fresh parsley or coriander, or one each
Half a kilogram brown or white flour
One teaspoon baking powder
Two teaspoons salt
Spices according to taste (pepper, ginger powder, garlic, cumin, for example)

1 First prepare the dough by sifting the flour with the baking powder, adding water gradually. It should be fairly stiff, but still elastic, with the consistency of pasta dough. Cover with a damp kitchen cloth.

2 Chop spring onions finely and mix with the finely-diced vegetables (or, for non-vegetarians, with minced meat), which have been mixed with the salt and spices.

3 Roll out ping-pong-sized balls of dough and fill with the mixture, forming it into the different shapes, either resembling *yamari*, round or crescent-shaped. Be sure they are fastened well, using some water so the mixture will not leak out while steaming.

4 Use a special *momo* steamer if available for the best result. Otherwise use a vegetable steamer or even boil them, thus producing a soup in the process, which can be served separately with the *momos*.

5 Steam for 15 minutes and test one first to see if it is ready, before removing all the *momos*.

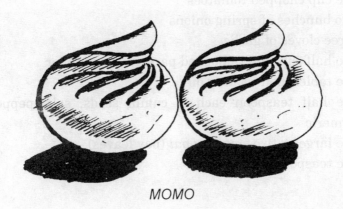

MOMO

## NINGRO TARKARI
### Bracken Fern Curry

Bracken fern is a seasonal vegetable of Nepal which grows in the wild prolifically during the rainy season. The entire stalk or, in the case of fat stalks, only the top half can be used. Normally to be found in marshy or shady wooded areas, if prepared correctly, it can be quite a delicacy, despite its somewhat limp, unappetising appearance. *Ningro* is a little bit reminiscent of asparagus, but is slightly gummy like lady fingers (which can substitute for fern in this recipe). Fern has to be carefully washed and its hard stems removed, though peeling is not usually required. Since it is harvested entirely in the wild, health food fans can rest assured that it is a fully organic vegetable, replete with essential iron and vitamins.

Two bunches of *ningro*
One cup chopped tomatoes
Two bunches of spring onions
Three cloves of garlic
One half cup finely chopped parsley or coriander
One tablespoon cooking oil
One half teaspoon each of cumin seeds, salt, pepper, turmeric
One large or two small *tej pat* (bay leaves)
One teaspoon salt

1 First prepare the fern by sorting out the tender from the hard stalks. Wash carefully and cut into one-inch pieces.

2 Chop up the tomatoes, spring onion and grate the garlic.

3 Heat the oil in a deep skillet, adding the cumin seeds and *tej pat* when hot.

4 When the seeds start to pop, add the fern and sautee covered on low heat for five minutes.

5 Add tomatoes and spices and mix well, sauteeing a further five minutes.

6 When the vegetables are done, at last, add the salt and parsley or coriander. Serve as a side dish with *dal-bhat*.

NINGRO

# FISH CURRY

Fish is considered a sign of good luck in Newar society and thus especially dried fish are offered to the deities. A pair of fish comprise one of the Asta Mangala of Mahayana Buddhism as practiced in Nepal. These eight auspicious symbols serving as a protective device are often seen painted around the entrances to Newari houses, are embossed on ritual items and figure on decorative banners.

Although Nepal is a land-locked country', as the Nepalese are fond of stressing, without access to the sea, yet its rivers abound with different kinds of fresh-water fish, a popular one being *rohu*. There is a large fish market in Kathmandu's Khicha Pokhari area, where fish mongers sell local and imported fish varieties. It is best to select a fish without too many bones, especially since Nepalese fish tend to abound with them.

One firm-fleshed fish
Half a cup of cooking oil, preferably mustard
One large onion
One green chilli
One cup chopped tomatoes
One teaspoon salt
Half a teaspoon each of turmeric, garam masala, chilli powder, pepper, to taste
One bunch of parsley or coriander

1 Cut a freshly-cleaned fish into small rounds or rectangular pieces and pat dry.
2 Heat oil in a deep skillet and fry the fish with a pinch of turmeric.
3 Remove from pan and, adding a bit more oil, fry chillies, chopped onions, garlic/ginger paste and other spices.
4 Add a bit more turmeric powder, salt and chopped tomatoes, plus half a cup of water to make a nice gravy.
5 Place the fish pieces in the mixture and cook for another five to ten minutes, depending upon the thickness of the fish.
6 Serve with chapatis or steamed rice.

*RITUAL KALAS*

# ALU-CHANNA TARKARI
## Potato-Chickpea Curry

This is a popular and classic dish in Nepal, amongst both Newars and non-Newars alike, though the preparation here is typically Newari, as can be noted by the addition of sesame. It can be considered a `Sunday luncheon' kind of dish which can be served with puris (small deep-fried chapatis) or rice. The usage of Kabuli channas - which are smaller and darker than the ordinary chickpeas - makes it a particularly rich source of protein and essential minerals, though somewhat harder to digest than the white chick peas.

Five large potatoes, peeled and cubed
Half a kilogram of chickpeas or Kabuli channas
Two large onions
One tablespoon ginger/garlic paste
Juice of one half lemon
Half a cup of sesame seeds (any colour)
One *tej pat* or bay leaf
One bunch of fresh coriander or parsley
Spices as desired: pepper, chilli powder, channa masala or garam masala
One teaspoon salt
Quarter of a cup of mustard oil

1 Soak channas overnight, especially if you are using Kabuli channas. The white ones only need to be soaked only four to six hours.

2 Boil together with potatoes in three cups of water, either in a pressure cooker (10 to 15 minutes) or in an ordinary saucepan, which will take double the time.

3 Pour oil into saucepan and fry the bay leaf or *tej pat*, adding ground and roasted sesame seeds, then the ginger/garlic paste and fry for a few minutes more.

4 Add salt and dry spices and mix everything into the channa and alu stew.

5 Pour in about two more cups of water and bring to a rapid boil.

6 At last, add chopped onions, tomatoes and lemon juice. and cook until done, about five minutes.

7 It is delicious served with yoghurt, especially if accompanied by puris.

MOMO STEAMER

# GWARCHA
## Newari Pasta - Bean Stew

The name alone renders this hearty stew Newari, despite the fact that it has a strong Tibetan influence. The dish itself originated out of the trade contacts between Tibetans and Newars, as the latter often used to trek overland to Lhasa and spend long periods there, due to the bad travel conditions. As it is very warming and filling, it is particularly recommended on a cold winter day or evening. Although it is possible to add meat (especially since both Tibetans and Newars are keen meat-eaters), this will not necessarily enhance its taste or nutritional value, which can be gauged from the numerous kinds of dried beans used.

*Gwarcha* can best be compared to an Italian bean and pasta stew, though with a distinctly oriental touch. Interestingly enough, Tibetan cuisine does not include ginger, so the Newars improvised when they thus adapted this dish to suite their own palates. Though most dishes in this book are for six people, this dish, in contrast, benefits from a wide culinary audience, and therefore the ingredients here are intended for at least 10 people.

One cup each of dried red kidney and soyabeans (fresh or dry)
One cup each of peas (fresh or dry) and (whole) black gram
Half a cup of chickpeas
One cup of string beans
One medium-sized cauliflower
One bunch of spinach
Two cups of minced cabbage
Three large onions
Half a kilogram of tomatoes
Two kilograms of brown flour
Half a cup of ginger/garlic paste
One tablespoon of cumin seeds
One heaping teaspoon of turmeric
Three cinnamon sticks
Four large *tej pat* or bay leaves
Half a cup of mustard oil
One tablespoon salt

1 Soak all dried beans overnight.
2 The following day, boil or pressure cook them together until nearly soft.
3 Add chopped cauliflower, spinach, cabbage, string beans, and any other seasonal vegetables (courgettes, for example), to the exclusion of the tomatoes.
4 Add the spices and garlic/ginger paste and simmer on low heat.
5 Knead brown or white flour and roll out as for a chapati, then cut into smallish, rectangular squares. Carefully slip into the stew, simmering a further 10 to 15

minutes, making sure they do not cling together while cooking.

6 Meanwhile, heat oil in a skillet and fry chopped onions, bay leaves and cumin seeds.

7 When the onions are browned, put in chopped tomatoes and add the mixture to the soup at the end.

8 You may serve this dish with soya sauce and/or vinegar for a slightly different flavour, if you so desire.

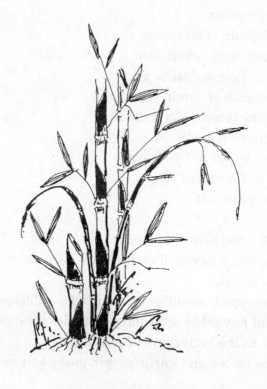

*BAMBOO BUSH*

# FAWSHI KWA
## Jackfruit *Tarkari*

Jackfruit is a seasonal vegetable grown in the southern Terai region of Nepal, which doubles as a fruit when it is very ripe. Then, its rough, brown surface conceals soft, yellow chunks of the luscious fruit hidden inside. Before reaching that stage, though, it is usually harvested in a firm, slightly raw condition and used as a vegetable. The following is a Newari version of a jackfruit curry, a recipe I learned from Amita Shakya, which is a fairly unusual dish, enjoyed only rarely, mainly due to the difficulties involved in handling the vegetable. The net result is, though, worth the trouble taken since it is a simultaneously savoury *and* healthy dish to boot.

Two small jackfruit (the large ones tend to be tough)
Two onions
One cup chopped tomato
One cup peas (optional)
One tablespoon *haji* (black sesame spice)
One and a half teaspoons of cumin seeds
One half teaspoon cinnamon powder
Two green chillies (optional)
One tablespoon ginger/garlic paste
One teaspoon turmeric
Two to three *tej pat* or bay leaves
Half a cup of brown sesame seeds
One teaspoon salt
One bunch of fresh coriander (or parsley)
Half a cup of mustard oil

1 Peel and cut up the jackfruit into small cubes [it is best to oil one's hands since this vegetable can be rather sticky in a raw state].

2 Parboil for about 20 minutes.

3 Heat oil to smoking stage in a karahi and add *tej pat, haji* and chopped onion, then the turmeric and garlic/ginger paste.

4 Add chopped tomato and other spices, frying for two to three minutes.

5 Add jackfruit and simmer another 10 to 15 minutes together with the peas, if you are using them. Add some water if it seems too dry.

6 When nearly ready, spinkle on the chopped coriander and serve as a side dish, possibly together with *alu-ko-achar*.

*FAWSHI*

# ALU-KO-ACHAR
## Potato Pickle

Nepal is known for its potato crop, which is continuously being improved through the input of developmental aid. For potato connoiseurs it is perhaps interesting to learn that the tastiest variety is grown in the highest altitudes, which I myself discovered while trekking in the Everest region. The potato dishes prepared in the trekkers' lodges, were, for that reason, a rare delicacy. In all parts of the country, though, the ubiquitous *alu* forms the base for the most numerous and popular *achars* (salads or pickles), to accompany chapatis and dal or *dal-bhat*. Otherwise as well, many *tarkari*, or vegetable preparations, are made with potatoes, of which there are basically two varieties, white and red-skinned. In the low lying areas like the Kathmandu Valley, Jerusalem's artichokes or *pindalu* (`village potato') can be substituted instead and are a delicious complement, especially when added to dal.

One kilogram potatoes
One cup sesame paste or tahini
One half cup whole sesame seeds
Half a cup fresh lemon juice
One tablespoon cooking oil
Two tablespoons fresh parsley or coriander
One half teaspoon each of salt, chilli powder, turmeric, green chillies, cumin seeds, mustard seeds (optional)

1 Parboil potatoes, peel and quarter.

2 Stir water into sesame paste, sesame seeds, lemon juice and salt, pour mixture over warm potatoes and mix until potatoes are nicely coated.

3 Heat oil and add dry spices, frying for a minute or two, being careful not to burn the spices.

4 Add to the potato mixture, together with the finely chopped parsley or coriander.

5 Stir slowly, without breaking the potato cubes, and serve either warm or cold as a side dish.

*KARUWA*

# CHUKAUNI
## Potato-Yoghurt Salad

This dish, a specialty of Palpa in far western Nepal, substitutes yoghurt for the mayonnaise commonly used in potato salad, with a superb result. It can be taken on a picnic or simply eaten as an accompaniment to other dishes.

Three large potatoes
One bunch of spring onions or one ordinary onion
One cup of yoghurt
One half teaspoon each of cumin, coriander, turmeric, chilli powder
One tablespoon of sesame seeds
Three cloves garlic
One teaspoon salt
Two tablespoons cooking oil

1 Boil potatoes, peel and allow to cool.
2 Dice the spring onion or onion and cut potatoes into cubes.
3 Mix in the yoghurt and stir well, being careful not to break the potatoes.
4 Heat the oil and fry the onions briefly, adding the spices and continuing to fry another minute or so.
5 Mix in the sesame seeds and add salt to taste.

## MOONG RA KARKALO
Moong paste wrapped in *karkalo* leaf

Though a little bit complicated to prepare, this dish stands as an unusual, highly nutritious side dish, to be served with *dal-bhat*, or any other main course. It was gleaned out of Ama Shrestha's repertory of Newari cuisine, which I was fortunate enough to enjoy at her house in Teku, Kathmandu.

Half a kilogram of split moong [black gram can also be used, if preferred]
A dozen tender, rolled *karkalo* leaves [in case of unavailability, preserved vine leaves in brine can, for example, be substituted]
One bunch of spring onions or one medium sized onion
One cup of chopped tomatoes
A pinch of turmeric, chilli powder, cumin, coriander, pepper
One tablespoon ginger/garlic paste
One teaspoon salt
One tablespoon mustard oil

1 Soak moong dal for several hours.
2 Wash the *karkalo* [Latin: colocasia] leaves carefully; if using vine leaves, take out of packet, wash and drain.
3 Drain and grind the dal, either using a grinding stone or a blender, to produce a smooth paste.
4 Blend the ginger and garlic paste, adding half a teaspoon salt, into the dal paste.
5 Put two teaspoons of the dal paste in the middle of a leaf and fold it into a rectangular roll.

6 Steam the roll for about five minutes, either in a vegetable or in a momo steamer.

7 Fry the chopped onion until golden [or, if using spring onion, only after frying the tomato], adding the tomatoes and dry spices, frying for a further two to three minutes.

8 Place the rolls carefully into the tomato mixture and simmer for a further five minutes, adding half a cup of water and salt to taste.

9 Serve either as an accompaniment of *dal-bhat*, with rice or even as a first course.

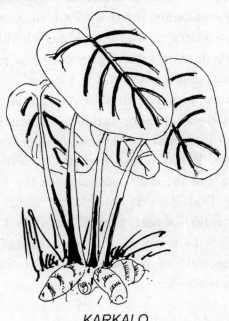

KARKALO

## MAKAI KI KODO KO DHIERU
### Grits or Millet Porridge

Though I have translated this dish as `porridge', it is not to be confused with an ordinary breakfast porridge, but rather has a porridge consistency and is served as a staple food, in place of rice or pasta. I first came accross *dhieru* while trekking in Nepal and was delighted to find this highly protein-laden alternative to rice, giving the trekker the extra energy needed to scale the peaks. However, as I recently found to my chagrin, it is becoming increasingly more difficult to locate a lodge which serves *dhieru* of whatever kind, whether maize or millet, on the normal trekking route. It is considered a "poor persons' diet", not suitable for *thulo manche*, the "big, important people", whether Nepalis or westerners. Hence, it is deemed more suitable for consumption by porters, who in Nepal can be either men or women as pictured here. It has been especially shown that under these circumstances, millet strengthens the body like no other single food item is capable of doing. *Makai* or maize *dhieru*, for its part, though considered more tasty than millet, is believed to give one a stomach ache, if excessive amounts of it are eaten, so it may best be consumed in moderation.

Two cups of corn flour [or grits], semolina or millet flour
Four cups of water
One teaspoon salt
One tablespoon butter or ghee [optional]

1 Boil the water and add salt, the butter or ghee.

2 Pour the sifted flour, semolina or grits into the water, little by little, stirring continuously.

3 Continue stirring until the flour coagulates into a smooth porridge, which usually takes from 10 to 15 minutes. Grits take slightly longer, generally the same time as rice.

4 Serve with a liquid stew, dal or even with yoghurt.

In Nepal, it is traditional to serve mustard greens sauteed in oil and garlic with the *dhieru*, accompanied by yoghurt, especially in the case of *makai ko dhieru*. For a richer alternative, substitute two of the cups of water for milk, which can be added towards the end.

*FEMALE BHARIYA*

## SWEET DISHES

### DUSHI MARI
Millet Cake

As can be noted by the presence of this recipe utilising the staple health food, millet, even the sweet dishes can be quite substantial in Nepal. There are, in fact, many kinds of bread products available in traditional Nepalese cuisine. Among them, millet cake is one kind prepared by Newars and non-Newars alike. Though millet is known as a poor man's food as has been shown, there is still no denying that it is a rich source of protein which in Nepali, is called *kodo roti*. The dish even harbours a healing dimension which was widely recognised until recent times. Up to approximately 20 years ago, *dushi mari* was prepared as a sacred food for the propitiation of the smallpox goddess, Sitala Mai. However, as this disease has been nearly eradicated now, these kinds of offerings are decreasing, regretably, along with the food culture they espoused.

One kilogram of millet flour
Half a cup of butter or ghee
Two eggs
One cup *shakar* or brown sugar
Half a liter milk
Two tablespoons coconut
Two tablespoons cashewnuts
One tablespoon almonds
Two to three drops vanilla
Two teaspoons baking powder

1 Sift the baking powder together with the millet flour and grate the coconut.

2 Beat the eggs and add milk.

3 Blend the sugar and butter until soft and add the milk solution together with the vanilla.

4 Mix everything together into a smooth batter and pour into a pre-fattened cake form.

5 Sprinkle dried fruit and coarsely chopped nuts on top and bake in a moderate oven for 30 to 45 minutes or until a fork inserted into the centre of the cake comes out clean.

6 Allow to cool before cutting it into squares or rectangles, to be served with afternoon tea or coffee.

NEWARI TEMPLE

# GAJAR KO HALWA
## Carrot Pudding

Two cups grated carrots
One half cup sugar (*shakar* or brown sugar is preferable to white)
A hand full of cashew nuts
Six cardamon pods
Half a cup of raisins [optional]
Half a liter milk
Half a cup butter or ghee

1 Wash, peel and grate carrots finely.
2 Fry in the ghee or butter until golden brown and add milk, sugar and spices.
3 Simmer for 10 to 15 minutes until the milk has coagulated and there is a lovely aroma and add raisins, if using them.
4 Spoon the *halwa* into a serving dish and sprinkle the chopped cashew nuts on top. Serve warm or cold, depending upon season.

*UKHU*

# HONEY COOKIES

Four tablespoons of honey
Two tablespoons of ghee
One piece of grated coconut
One-inch piece of grated ginger
A few cloves to taste

1 Melt ghee in saucepan and add honey, together with grated coconut, ginger and cloves.
2 When the mixture cools, form into bars or into round cookies.
3 Serve as snacks or with afternoon tea or coffee.

## SIKWNI
### Yoghurt Dessert

One liter milk
Four tablespoons sugar
Two tablespoons yoghurt
Half cup of coconut powder
Ten peanuts, finely ground

1 Boil milk for 20 minutes, making sure it does not burn.
2 Allow to cool down until tepid and mix in sugar, yogurt, coconut and peanut powder.
3 Cover with a thick cloth and leave for five hours before serving.
4 In the summer, it is advisable to refrigerate it for some time before serving.

## MAKAI KO HALUWA
### Maize Pudding

This may be considered a sweet version of *dhieru*, which can also be used as a breakfast food, especially since it is a source of quick energy.

One cup of maize grits
One cup of *shakar* or brown sugar
One quarter cup of ghee or butter
One tablespoon of coconut, powdered or grated
Two pods of cardamon

1 Clean and wash the grits, then drain off excess water.
2 Heat butter or ghee in a saucepan and add grits, stirring well.
3 When they start to brown, add the milk, sugar, coconut and cardamon.
4 Simmer for ten minutes, or until the grits are soft.
5 Although normally served warm, this *haluwa* can also be eaten cold in the summer.

*MAKAI*

# KHIR
## Rice Pudding

This is perhaps the most popular of all Nepalese sweet dishes and figures as an important offering in all manner of religious ceremonies. The version of *khir* presented here is a relatively basic one, though for a more colesterol-laden one, substitute half the milk for cream. Mashed pumpkin pulp can be substituted for rice, to make *pharsi-ko-khir*.

One cup of rice
One liter of milk
Four teaspoons of ghee or butter
Four teaspoons of brown sugar or *shakar*
Cardamon, coconut, raisins, cashew nuts, pistacio nuts, almond slivers, as desired

1 Clean and wash the rice thoroughly, drain and fry in the ghee or (unsalted) butter.
2 Boil milk and pour half of it into another pot.
3 Add the rice to the milk left on the stove and stir frequently while it is simmering.
4 Add the rest of the milk when the rice is nearly ready, little by little, stirring all the while, to prevent burning.
5 Now add the sugar, a few cardamon pods, grated coconut, chopped cashew nuts and raisins (if desired).
6 Serve in a deep bowl, sprinkling some chopped pistacio nuts on the top.
7 *Khir* can be eaten either warm or cold as a dessert, a snack or even a breakfast food.

## HALUWA
### Coconut Fudge

This is the most basic *haluwa*, easy to prepare, but still very popular and tasty.

Four cups of *suji* flour [semolina]
Half a cup of ghee or butter
Half a cup of sugar (*shakar* or brown sugar is best)
One cup of grated coconut

1 Heat the ghee or (unsalted) butter in a large saucepan.
2 Gradually pour in the semolina and fry it gently for five minutes.
3 Add sugar and coconut and fry for another two to three minutes.
4 *Haluwa* can be eaten either hot or cold.

## JIRHI
### Nepalese Doughnuts

*Jirhi* is considered a sweet for festive occasions in Nepal, known for its gooey, sugary sweetness and is considered compulsory for rounding off a feast with. Although called a doughnut' due to its round shape, it is, however, less of one than *sel*, for example, since it is not dry, but rather dripping with a sugary solution.

Five cups of white flour [whole wheat is not be suitable for this dish]
Three cups of sugar
Two cups of cooking oil
One tablespoon of baking soda

1 Sift flour together with the baking soda and beat to a smooth batter by adding three cups of water gradually.

2 Cover and leave overnight.

3 When ready to make the *jirhi*, first prepare the sweet solution by bringing two cups of water and three cups of sugar to boil.

4 Cook for 20 minutes until it has become a sticky solution.

5 Heat the oil in a deep frying pan, karahi or a wok.

6 Use a pastry-maker (same as for *sel*) and squeeze the batter through it into the oil, in a round, squiggly shape.

7 Stir gently with a perforated spoon, turn over once and remove after about five minutes.

8 Place the *jirhi* into the sweet solution, pressing gently for a minute or two.

9 Serve either warm or cold.

*JIRHI*

# LAKHAMARI
## Black Gram and Rice Flour Biscuits

*Lakhamari* is a traditional ceremonial sweet within the Newar community, which, similarly to *yamari*, is reputed to be centuries old. Especially prior to the advent of Indian sweet shops supplying most people's needs today, *lakhamari* was the biscuit people were fondest of preparing and serving to their "most honoured guests" and relatives. It was particularly used as a way for the parents of the bride to announce their daughter's wedding: they would distribute the *lakhamari* instead of wedding invitations! Either a large version, resembling a huge, round biscuit would be prepared, or the smaller, twisted version featured here. In the case of the former, pieces would be broken off and distributed, larger ones going to the closer relatives. Nowadays, it is mostly sweet shops which produce *lakhamari* and people buy them there. However, if you happen to have plenty of time on your hands and feel like making a special effort to practice a nearly lost art, you will be richly rewarded for having produced a sweet which is simultaneously traditional and delicious.

One kilogram rice flour [or two-thirds rice and one third whole wheat flour, for a heartier version]
One teaspoon baking powder
Half a cup of ghee or butter
A cup of split black gram
Half a kilogram of sugar [*shakar* is ideal for this sweet]
Two tablespoons of powdered sugar [optional]
Two cups of cooking oil